Those People

Paul Stephenson

smith|doorstop

Published 2015 by
smith|doorstop Books
The Poetry Business
Bank Street Arts
32–40 Bank Street
Sheffield S1 2DS

Copyright © Paul Stephenson 2015
All Rights Reserved

ISBN 978-1-910367-51-3
Typeset by Utter
Printed by People for Print, Sheffield

Acknowledgements
Thanks to the editors of the following publications in which versions of some of these poems first appeared: *Café Writers*, *Lighthouse*, *Magma*, *The North*, *Poetry News*, *Smiths Knoll*, *South Bank Poetry*, *Swimming Lessons* (Jerwood/Arvon anthology). The first line of 'Birthday Cards' is inspired by Ted Kooser's poem 'Father'. 'Angle End' adopts the form of Mona Arshi's poem 'On Ellington Road'.

smith|doorstop Books are a member of Inpress: www.inpressbooks.co.uk. Distributed by Central Books Ltd., 99 Wallis Road, London E9 5LN

The Poetry Business is an Arts Council
National Portfolio Organisation

Contents

5	Roget
6	Do You Have Any Questions?
7	Birthday Cards
8	The Guest
9	Wake Up And
10	Arrangements
11	Angle End
13	Gare du Midi
14	Cab
15	Telescope
16	Passwords
17	School for Dummies
19	Glacé
20	Duffle
21	Shopping
22	Ashby-de-la-Zouch
23	Two Tannoys (A Noise Annoys)
24	The Seventies
25	Those People
26	Managing a Width
27	Round the Block
29	The Pull
30	Capacity

Roget

At first glance I took it for a being –
some kind of dinosaur, like the ones I knew
who ran and roared and clawed,
flattening ferns, making the earth shudder,
ripping off flesh and devouring each other.

I opened it up, protecting the spine.
There were long terms and new ways to describe,
complicated doing words never seen before
or scratched by teacher's prehistoric hands
on the green blackboard.

I thought I saw *The Saurus*.

Do You Have Any Questions?

What do we do with coats?
How much time will we have?
Can we finish our sentence?
Where are we meant to hang them?
Should we leave them outside?
How will they know it's us?
How much do we need to score?
What if we've two the same day?
Will anything get taken off?
Have we got to answer them all?
What if we want the toilet?
Will there be scrap paper?
What if we're feeling ill?
If we don't know do we guess?
How many can we get wrong?
How much do we have to write?
Can we use both sides?
Are dictionaries okay?
Should we put our names?
How do we know where to sit?
What if we lose our number?
What if we forget our number?
Can we leave when we want to?
Should we learn everything?
What if we go completely blank?
Do we have to wait till the end?
Can we skip any questions?
Can we take away the questions?
Will we get last year's questions?

Birthday Cards

Today you'd be seventy if you hadn't been
so overweight. We'd all be sending you
funny birthday cards with cartoons of fat men
up to no good in their shed, or dozed off
in a deckchair, fingers laced over their belly.

There'd be a dog pushing a lawn mower,
going round and round a rotary washing line
of women's smalls while the rope leash unwinds,
well-trained to cut increasing circles of grass
and with no energy spent on the fat man's part.

I can see the joke about the huge naked bloke
who hasn't seen his genitals in years
wheeling his stomach in a wheelbarrow.
Greetings would come with exclamations marks
cos fat men are fond of making loud remarks.

Or else, relatives of fat men like to exclaim,
not enough to simply say, with best wishes,
lots of love and kisses, 'Happy Birthday'.
You'd open mine from your chair and laugh,
say 'Bloody cheek!', stand it next to the other.

Today, I spend my lunch hours in June
browsing Clintons, Smiths, Paperchase,
picking out big laughs in cellophane.
I find the silliest, rudest, fattest one to send,
doing my best to get hold of you.

The Guest

I'll never know who he was,
the man that just sat there,

his face pressed into the head rest,
his beard a black avalanche.

He sat there in the way
piles of gravel do, delivered

to the beginning of a drive,
one ear folded like a landscape

Christmas card, one eye
a red foil bauble

dented from storage.
He sat in the glow of the lights

and we prodded him
with the fire poker, tickled

his nose with a strip
of gold tinsel. Nothing.

In the kitchen, cold meats, pickles.
Upstairs, choices to be made.

Wake Up And

smell the coffee
smell the coughing
the cacophony
the cafard
the cavern

wake up and smell Cavafy
wake up and smell Cefalonia

smell the kaftan
smell the kif
the köfte
the Kiefer
the O'Keeffe

wake up and smell the cufflink
wake up and smell the coffin

Arrangements

Me and my grandfather admire the pheasant.
We are expecting a local undertaker.

Mr Purkiss is punctual. He barely rings once.
His face is bowed, his hair brilliantined down.

He finds an apology, carries his condolences
across the threshold, twice wiping his shiny

black pointed feet. His look cannot be
more serious, but then seriousness

at the end of the day is his family business.
We whisper tidy sentences and agree

on something. And on nothing. He lays down
his plastic binder of veneers and finishes,

assures us his wife, Amanda, normally Mandy,
will be on hand for every eventuality.

The Windsor and Harrogate are both popular.
Blue mist. Mountain cherry. There is no hurry.

He must be going, standing, walking backwards,
gone. Me and my grandfather explode with laughter.

Angle End

Mr and Mrs Pagan and their Great Dane, Solomon, always mowing their many acres but not using them for anything, even running on.

Jock Mappledorum who watched the cricket asleep.

Elsie Merrick who cleaned the primary school and never took her apron off.

Professor Wright who cycled seven miles to work and back each day, then one day only made it six miles.

Poddy Ablett, shaped like a ball, who lived inside the boarded-up Sunday School.

Coral Scase who got annoyed if I wanted two ounces and two ounces instead of four ounces.

Ben and Brigitta. She was Swedish. Actually Birgitta.

The Bilbys who did up the Old Vicarage. Dr Bilby who gave me 50p for Bob-a-Job after I moved a ton of bricks from one corner of his drive to the other.

Shirley Armstrong and her husband The Pope who never threw the ball back.

Tom and Adam Long whose Dad was in Hong Kong.

The Heyworth-Harmers who made pop-up Christmas cards each year and sent one to my grandparents because they'd lived in their house before they did.

Mrs Bullock who left her change in a Tower of Pisa just inside her porch.

Pippa Beaumont whose horse vanished overnight.

Denise and Danny Joslin who ran the Country & Western. Their daughter Karen I went to Calais and back with in a day.

Lady Duffus whose robbers ate her bananas and left their skins.

Percy Waters who dug up whatever you wanted as long as you took your own bag.

Caroline Gardiner who'd played chess with Lady Diana.

The Reverend Rodbard who passed round Smarties on a pewter platter.

Bev Warnock on the fruit machine who elbowed you if you got too close when she had flashing nudges.

Meredith Marsh and her refurbished dovecote.

John Driver who ran the village pub while also teaching at a secondary school in London.

Gare du Midi

You are going in London yes in London?
I am going to London, to England, to London
English people very kind very friendly in London
Queen is living Bucking Ham Palace London
I go with you today travel in London

It is difficult to go with me to London
How you go there today in London?
By train, I am going by train to London
England embassy giving papers London
My sister was going she did go in London

Is possibly you know her she famous in London?
Brussels is cosmopolitan and big like London
How much time is train to go in London?
The train is fast, it takes two hours to London
Show me please where train go in London

Always they looking passport for go in London?
You must show a passport and a ticket for London
Papers and people are difficult in London
There are many cameras and policemen in London
It is crowded, busy and stressful in London

My sister they not love her I need go in London
You say we friends for enter train in London
You say we holidays in London
I dream buses visit Tower of London
I must go in London I am happy London

Cab

My mother tells me to ask
for a reliable driver.
She says apparently
this is what to mention
because Jill told her
over a pensioner's lunch.

Jill learnt it from her Ron
who was chatting Friday
with Mick up the Five Bells,
and Mick should know
after a good thirty years
working the rank.

My mother says when you ring,
especially at night,
to emphasise the *reliable*
and they'll understand
right away on the other end
what you're on about.

Telescope

On clear nights,
not a stone-throwing youth in sight,
Diabetic Fred to our left
kicks out legs, extends the neck
of his own contraption: a miraculous,
mechanical, mongrel invention
concocted from left behind lenses –
an all-nighter leaning over,
rifling, torching, welding, fitting,
the bare bulb dangling.

He knocks using the knocker,
calls us to the pavement
to squint a look, twist until sharp.
We take turns marvelling
in our street's planetarium
at the full button moon
with hairline crack.

Next day on the doorstep
Fred sits in bandaged sandals,
as if nothing cosmic has ever
happened between us, blows
through a descant recorder
to his own tune, with ten fingers,
eight toes and one eye clouding over.

Passwords

I avoid the house I grew up in,
keep away from my mother

and father's birthdays: calendar
opposites, June and January.

I steer clear of my brother's
crash, rule out the hot summer

I left school, graduated, went off.
I adopt different characters,

mix upper and lower case.
I do my utmost to never

choose when I was born.
Mine take years to crack.

School for Dummies

History	Conquerors came. Conquerors saw. Conquerors played conkers.
Geography	People populate the place melting and meandering.
Sociology	The class system begins at school. Children try to fit in.
Biology	Birds. Bees. Bedfordshire. Nine months, but more for an elephant.
Physics	What goes up must come down. Attraction, repulsion or both.
Chemistry	You can't eat your dinner off a periodic table.
Latin	Cicero, Virgil, Ovid, then Curriculum Vitae.
Greek	A god for everything, even animal husbandry.
French	Masculine or feminine. In doubt, go with your instincts.
German	Goethe and Young Werther. Not louts, umlauts. Endings matter.

Art	Keep things in perspective.
	Start dark, get lighter. Don't smudge it.
Music	Every good boy deserves football,
	every bad boy punk rock.
English	Much ado on balconies.
	Suicide as you like it.
Maths	Less is definitely not more.
	It all adds up to not much.

Glacé

Fact is there are no facts
but if there were, then once
in an issue of *Smash Hits* I read
Madonna hates glacé cherries.
You can imagine her predicament
when it comes to cakes and cocktails
and, sometimes, on top of trifles.
She's wary of glacé, never blasé.
Her doo-wop style pop shuffle
and third single from Like a Prayer
was called *Cherish*, not *Cherries*,
the one where in the video
she's writhing on the sand,
ravished by the ocean – don't ask
me which ocean: the waves lapped
and there was foam. Pacific?
As for candied fruit generally,
she can't see the point, but then
nor can I, if I can be candid.
Once a year it comes in a hamper
made of wicker you must sign for,
and which takes up space. Some jar
of yellow and orange bits in syrup.
I want to say 'topaz'.
Topaz.
Bitter. Inedible. Mostly unopenable.
But then Kylie Minogue dislikes
thick-sliced wholemeal Hovis loaves.

Duffle
i.m. Eve Greenwood

Dear Eve, last night you confessed
you had recently been right
round central London on foot
looking out for duffles, simply to know

how much one goes for nowadays,
and been taken aback by the fact
the young shop assistant who approached you
had never heard of such a proper coat.

On Old Bond Street your discovery
they can fetch upwards of two hundred pounds
has not convinced you to ask more than twenty
given the current climate.

You asked me if I know how eBay works,
pledging to make it your mission,
apart from chucking out this winter,
to get web-wise and do *collect only*.

This is to tell you, Eve, I have seen a man
today on the train with toggles.
He undid them then sat in front of me
but looked nothing whatsoever like Nigel.

Shopping

Well, I could do with more Hughs,
a few more more expensive Hughs.
Grant and Laurie are two-a-penny.

Brains are a no-brainer, they're on the list,
as are the piano symphonies of Liszt.

I wouldn't say no to a dozen fresh distances,
and if, on your travels, a jar of far-flung.

Theories by Adorno to adorn my wall
and maybe some of that Ancient Egypt.

I think I'm alright for sponsored runs.
I'm actually drowning in good intentions.
I don't need bicarbonate of anything.

Ashby-de-la-Zouch

They're a bit Belgian –
the town's people mooch for hours
until it begins: the summer sale on
mini-breaks in Asda lift shafts, dashing
to trap index fingers in revolving
doors. The men mostly choose

to work at Deloitte & Touche, drink
Tizer-on-the-rocks, Sundays compete
in ouch!-shouting contests, carry shabby
satin pouches packed with cinders of papers
perused. The chiselled women wear smiles
like snagged zips and la-di-da brooches
confectioned from bashful cockroaches.

The children (all called Zoë or Zack)
are cashed in at twelve, dropped off
in lay-bys wearing width fitting shoes.
They spend their teenage years crouched
over and bent, blowing oxygen onto the
kindling of GCSE French. As such,

slovenly couples are quids-in but don't
touch much – to avoid rashes; hubbies
walk grouchy pooches past the zoo;
the missus collects vouchers for free minutes
redeemable Shrove Tuesdays for slouching
in show homes on charcoal couches to watch
The Sound of Music together on mute.

Two Tannoys (A Noise Annoys)

If you see *fuse* anything *knee*
suspicious please *sheepish*
report it *sleaze rear poor*
tit immediately *mead*
to a *idiot* member
wham of *ember*
railway staff
ale waist
fast.

Attention!
Train *tension*
rain approaching
nap pro. Chimp please
stand *plead* well *land* back
elbow whack from the *crumb*
platform edge *Plath morph rat fed.*

The Seventies

Colonels had kittens contemplating pounds and pence,
spent half their holiday hanging around Dover.

> Singers saved their kisses for me
> but inflation was humiliating.

> Nobody buckled up.
> Everyone had beards.

> Bell-ringers wore bell-bottoms
> and A to B was by space hopper.

Bin men slept in as rats binged on rubbish.
A brouhaha broke out over women in the Wimpy.

Those People

What are they called? Those people who turn up
unfashionably early, too premature for it to be a party,
just a room full of drinks and square metres of carpet.
I mean the opposite of stragglers, not the hard core
with staying power and no home to go to, or the dregs
of the party who've no intention of going anywhere
but love to linger, end up getting chucked out into
the night, or if they're lucky and it's a good party,
into a warm sunrise. I'm talking eager beavers,
the party-goers who make a punctual appearance,
greeted at the door by hosts running around with
nibbles still in cupboards and half their face on,
the guests who arrive bang on and get shown through
to hover admiring the smoothness of wallpaper,
which they do politely, not entering yet into the spirit
of the party, swaying by a bucket of orange punch.
Those folk who don't often get to go to parties,
so have it marked fluorescent for weeks in their diary
and make a mission of what to wear, but never sure
of the dress code, opt to play it safe and wear jeans.
Those characters who eight hours later could be
hitting Havana, sipping mojitos and dancing mambo
and rumba and salsa merengue with dollar-hungry
doppelgängers of Che Guevara in desperate need
of mechanical parts for dilapidated Dodges and
Chevrolets, but hey, instead revel in the refuge
of empty strip-lit galley kitchens, to sit on a ledge
of marbled Formica, slurring into sausage rolls
and spilling their life, is there a name for them?

Managing a Width

The man with the dreads contract cleans.
Once in a while he uploads his muscles.
He posts his pecs, claiming they're natural.
Such a horrid, swollen, oversized chest!

As a small boy he stuck to the shallow end.
When he didn't lob his thick foam float,
he grasped it, kicked with all his puny might.
He wet his hair, the pretty water rat.

In technical drawing, afternoon register.
Each lesson Mr Fuller called out 'Rory'.
Cory, without fail, would answer 'Here'.
We waited for it. It never wasn't funny.

I scroll his locks, so blonde and matted.
He lives by the roundabout, says kids rib him.
Perhaps abs today, tomorrow gluts.
He's building up, becoming his own hero.

Round the Block

My default was anti-clockwise:
fourteen minutes on go-slow
but under ten when legging it.
Straight down the crazy paving
and first base the Post Office
to check on ads for babysitting,
past the village Memorial Hall
where they held the whist, bingo,
fête, fruit and vegetable show,
then the Blue Seat by the nettles
at the far edge of the rec' and
in through the heavy latch gate,
passing alongside Grandad who
loved his jazz, a quick squizz
for fresh-dug mounds of earth
and flowers among the molehills,
striding the loud gravel sloping
entrance of St. Nicholas' church
and out at the Old People's Flats,
taking in Whitethorn's dark thatch,
peering into the Victorian primary
and Mr Lamper's junior class,
skirting the fence at Mrs Bulgar's,
always ninety-three or ninety-four,
to Oulton House and Iceni Cottage,
the slide, swings and roundabout,
not forgetting the short dinner lady's
wonky table of pickles and chutneys,
her deck chair and rattling jam jar,

curving left at the grass triangle
that gave distances to next places,
spotting the carved wooden sign
with its hare and pheasant staring
out against the cornfield relief
each side of Queen Wilburga,
and further, back to the Roman
Road, Butt Lane, mud and cow
parsley running wild for miles,
to catch Dad standing there,
the tan leather of the leash
dangling, the dog long gone.

The Pull

Moon is a dare:

a raid on a haystack,
a stock of silver,
a salver of harvest,
a hay vest of gathered

together field;

the fold's reflection,
the flock's reflex,
the heart's flux,
elected flicker.

Capacity

Seventy litres: in theory more than plenty
for three t-shirts, two shorts, the pair of jeans
you're wearing. Then the question of the tent,

saucepan, small canister of gas, map and bible
of Thomas Cook timetables – every single train
possibility from here to Ankara. One crisp fifty

thousand lira note, a handful of Swiss francs
and wad of American Express traveller's cheques.
Foreign currency kept flat, zipped inside a canvas

wallet with Velcro strap, wrapped tight around
the waist. Typical Monday. Your father at work.
Your mother out somewhere. Your lift here soon.